AF447356

THE BOY IN AMAZON'S VR CINEPLEX APP

'Emerging from Trafficking. Evolving into a New Era'

JOEL PETER BROWN

JOEL
FLICKSTEIN
SPECIAL GUEST
MILES
LAVERTY
A JOEL BROWN FLIXTEXTING STORY
HIS HAUNTING IS HIS ONLY
ESCAPE FROM CAPTIVITY
THE BOY IN AMAZON'S
VR CINEPLEX APP
DIRECTED BY
JOEL BROWN
SCREENPLAY BY
JOEL BROWN
STORY BY
JOEL BROWN
STUDIOBINDER PRESENTS A STUDIOBINDER PRODUCTION IN ASSOCIATION WITH STUDIO PB ACTOR NAME ACTOR NAME "MOVIE TITLE"
CASTING BY CASTING CREW MUSIC BY COMPOSER COSTUME DESIGNER COSTUME DESIGNER EDITED BY EDITOR PRODUCTION DESIGNER PRODUCTION DESIGNER PRODUCED BY PRODUCER
DIRECTOR OF PHOTOGRAPHY DIRECTOR OF PHOTOGRAPHY CO-EXECUTIVE PRODUCER CO-EXECUTIVE PRODUCER EXECUTIVE PRODUCER EXECUTIVE PRODUCER
QMYSTERY BEGINS   SUMMER 2022
A WORD-OF-MOUTH URBAN LEGEND

DEDICATION

Right then. Before we start, I'd like
introduce the band.

My all-in-all God-the father, God-the Son -
Jesus Christ and God-the Holy Spirit.

My mother, Sheila M Brown.

Jerusalem and Israel

Ukraine and Russia

An 11-years-old Russian/Palestinian from
Star, Kedah who's known as Miles Laverty

Kindle Amazon Publishing

Amazon Prime VR Movie Theater Experience

THE PARAMOUNT THEATER
The movie theatre has been a much-needed
refuge during times of trouble....During the
Depression, viewers were swept away by the sunny-
natured Shirley Temple, making them forget
about their troubles for a while. It was farewell
to all the worries and cares of the day. When the

PARAMOUNT THEATER opened its doors, we forgot about names like Hitler and Mussolini. It was time instead to unwind and dream a little. The PARAMOUNT introduced new young singers like Frank Sinatra, and showed films with big stars like Clark Gable and Betty Hutton. These were the times that tried men's souls, but the glitz and glamour of Hollywood kept us distracted and entertained. We retained our perspective, and most importantly, allowed ourselves to hold on, to our national sense of humor.

THE 4-STAR THEATER

4-Star Theater is located on Clement Street, an iconic location for the film industry. Clement Street has been part of San Francisco' s diverse movie culture for many generations, particularly known for also showing Asian and art films.

All neighbors within the 74145 zip code who are outside of the faith. I am begging God for the day that we can worship him together. Father, we ask You to fill our heart with Your love for others. We hold 74145 up to You and beg for them to see the truth about Your Son Jesus (Ro. 9:2-3).

And for all who I havee not mentioned who bought this book that I don't know your name to mention, you're not forgotten, please sign your name below:

_________________________.

As I just want you encourage you all by saying…

You are a window of possibility and future. You are a ray of sunshine that gleams hope on a gloomy day. You are a bright forecast that let's you know there will be and expected end, even when things don't look good. You have a wild imagination and mountain moving faith. You are an appreciation of beauty & excellence.You are one of my heroes.

You're worth more than GOLD!

Don't let anyone tell you you're not loved!

So never let anyone tell you you're not good enough!

We all have days we feel like we're messed up, but the truth is that we are all diamonds in the ruff! No matter what people have said, you're worth more than GOLD!

You're a superhero because I see you as one, even if no one does.

So be your own superhero because Marvel and DC has already taken all the others that everyone is trying to be.

To prove you are a superhero, ask yourself what obstacles have you pushed through? Then ponder what Christopher Reeves, Superman had once stated when he said that "A hero is an ordinary individual who finds the strength to persevere and endure inspire of overwhelming obstacles." If you don't see yourself as one, despite that quote from a superhero, then reminisce all the times you have helped people and animals as you ponder what Stan Lee said, "That a person who helps others simply because it should or must be done, and because it is the right thing to do, is indeed without a doubt, a real hero!"

I want to call out the hero in you through this and say you are a hero, yet an impossibility in an impossible world that is setting an example for your generation!

For we are saved by hope: but hope that is seen is not hope: for what a man sees, why do he yet hope for? What better way to be a hero than to be hope for someone through whatever means being talents or gifts, so don't ask yourself what the world wants. Ask yourself what makes you come alive, and go do that, because what the world wants is people who have come alive. Go set yourself on fire with it, and people will come to watch you burn.

I BELIEVE IN YOU!

"You are here on purpose because you have a purpose you, your heart is open, your mind is ready to receive because God is not finished with you yet, your best days are right in front of you, and you have victory in your life, because Jesus love you."
– Pastor Paul Daugherty

CONTENTS

CONTENTS

ACKNOWLEDGMENTS

Remember the agreement you made with us. Violent enemies are hiding in every dark corner of the earth.
[Psalm 74:20]

"In our child trafficking prevention curriculum, Not a Number, we address vulnerabilities – things like rejection from family, addiction, mental illness, bullying, low self-esteem, and previous sexual victimization. There are organizations across the U.S. that have facilitators bringing Not a Number curriculum to young people in their communities. They work to build trust with youth while giving them opportunities to bravely talk about what they're going through."
- Love 146, love146.org

Fact. Child trafficking affects every country in the world, including the United States. Children make up 27% of all human trafficking victims worldwide, and two out of every three identified child victims are girls

FACT: A majority of the time, victims are trafficked by someone they know, such as a friend, family member or romantic partner.

FACT: Boys and men are just as likely to be victims of human trafficking as girls and women. However, they are less likely to be identified and reported. Girls and boys are often subject to different types of trafficking, for instance, girls may be trafficked for forced marriage and sexual exploitation, while boys may be trafficked for forced labor or recruitment into armed groups.

FACT: Human trafficking can include forced labor, domestic servitude, organ trafficking, debt bondage, recruitment of children as child soldiers, and/or sex trafficking and forced prostitution.

FACT: Human trafficking is not the same thing as smuggling, which are two terms that are commonly confused. Trafficking does not require movement across borders. In fact, in some cases, a child could be trafficked and exploited from their own home. In the U.S., trafficking most frequently occurs at hotels, motels, truck stops and online.

FACT: Trafficking can involve force, but people can also be trafficked through threats, coercion, or deception. People in trafficking situations can be controlled through drug addiction, violent relationships, manipulation, lack of financial independence, or isolation from family or friends, in addition to physical restraint or harm.

FACT: Trafficking occurs all over the world, though

the most common forms of trafficking can differ by country. The United States is one of the most active sex trafficking countries in the world, where exploitation of trafficking victims occurs in cities, suburban and rural areas. Labor trafficking occurs in the U.S., but at lower rates than most developing countries.

If you suspect someone is a victim of trafficking, contact the National Human Trafficking Resource Center at 1-800-373-7888. The confidential hotline is open 24 hours a day, every day, and helps identify, protect and serve victims of trafficking.

THIS IS THE BEGINNING OF THE
END of child trafficking.

"The phrase "human trafficking" was introduced decades ago with relatively few people tracking the issue. But today, many of us know about this horrific crime. The number of reports about children being trafficked is skyrocketing. It can seem like the issue is getting worse as new stories are unearthed. But the more deeply we understandably the issue of child trafficking, the closer we are to ending it." - Love 146, love146.org

"The trafficking of children will end when our collective expectations of what is possible, what is just, and what is effective have been reoriented." - Love 146, love146.org

"It always seems impossible until it's done."

- NELSON MANDELA

WORDS FROM CHILDREN IN LOVE
146'S SURVIVOR CARE

*"This program gives us someone to trust,
especially if we have been in 'the life.' There's
no judgment. I can talk to her about anything,
and if I need help, she's there."*
A 16-YEAR-OLD IN OUR SURVIVOR CARE

*"As a young teen, I was lured into the life. After a while,
I lost view of who I once was. I couldn't see any other
path to take other than the one my pimp was offering
me, I was about to give up but then out of nowhere, I
was given light and a way out when I met Love146."*
A 17-YEAR-OLD IN OUR SURVIVOR CARE

*"You can meet people who are willing to love
and understand you without asking for any
money or things in return. Be strong and don't
lose hope because you'll find the right path."*
A 10-YEAR-OLD IN OUR SURVIVOR CARE

*"Education is just like a weapon that protects a
person. When I finish my studies, I will also be
able to raise my family from poverty and I can
also protect myself from bad people because I
can distinguish between right and wrong."*
A 13-YEAR-OLD IN OUR SURVIVOR CARE

*"I want to become a defender of the oppressed. I've
experienced being oppressed, that's why I don't*

want other children to go through it. I realize I'm fortunate because I was given the opportunity and chance to change my life and other people's lives."
A 10-YEAR-OLD IN OUR SURVIVOR CARE

Sources: [i] Give Her a Choice: Building A Better Future For Girls (Save the Children). [ii] United Nations Office on Drug and Crime

FOREWARD

A Love Letter to Amazon Prime and Publishing:

I know it's not Valentine's Day but Valentine's Day shouldn't be just a generous holiday of love for one day, but each day should be treated as Valentine's Day; as you never know who you might touch with a simple act of kindness.

And while many people celebrate the gift of love once a year in spite of various Valentine traditions have been associated with the celebration of Valentines, and different cultures celebrate different ways. I thought it was high time that a writer like me celebrate my love for a service like yours that gives hope to writers.

After all, as a writer we probably spend more time working on nurturing the best within ourselves than any relationship! So, I decided to write a love letter to your company, Amazon while I Write My Love Letter to my writing business. Please feel free to share this with all you wish on your staff who might be touched.

Dear Amazon Publishing,

You know, the Art of giving is to be in service as a Writer, through my craft I have the ability to inspire change in people; its a tool to change people's out-look and to give them something to better themselves with as I also get to Connect with People, Walk in their Shoe, and Flip-the-Script to change the scene for a day in hope that it might change the outcome that might be bad to turn it around for the good with because stories give hope, hope gives possibilities, possibilities freedom - the pen is mightier than the sword!

I want to express my love and gratitude to you.

You have fulfilled a missing piece in my heart.

And you've become a big part in my heart.
I have journeyed many roads:
- Some have been smooth.
- Some have been bumpy.
- All have been worth it, even the ones that left me empty handed that taught me how its better to give than to get what's coming to you, and life is about enjoying the journey over than being at the destination.

I have experienced incredible highs balanced by

tear-full lows.

You have always "kept me in check" so that I don't take anything for granted. I've learned that what gets taken for granted gets taken away.

I've learned more about what it takes to be your partner in the art of writing than I could have ever imagined.

And I am better for it.

You have taught me a lot about myself.

And I am better for it.

Mostly, you have taught me that I am enough. I am brave enough, strong as a mule enough, strong enough and smart enough to do "you". And your rewards never cease to surprise and amaze me. Thank you. Thank you for standing by me during my breakdowns and breakthroughs in my endeavors during process to getting a book published to meet an audience where they are at.

I promise you that I will grow and get better by continuing to invest in and work on myself as I help people to be the best that they can be when they are at their worst.

I promise not to take you for granted ... nor all the people that support and help me through the Kindle Direct Amazon Publishing.

I promise to stretch beyond what's comfortable

in the spirit of moving our excellent word together forward.

AND, FINALLY, I promise to keep loving you as the laborer that you are.

Faithfully your with love,

Joel

P. S. - Today I've learned how Your Service (Whatever it is whether big or small) to another is a Reflection of You As a Strong Heart Leads to a Healthy Service, in order to achieve and sustain good health, you aught to love yourself first. If you don't think you're worth the effort to lead a healthy lifestyle, then why should anyone else value you? Taking that a step further, how could you have a successful service if you don't love yourself first? Your service is a reflection of you. If you are suffering, so too will your service. Your service longs for you to have stamina, strength and clarity to thrive. These demands are hard to achieve when you coming from a place of depletion. If you don't love yourself first, both you and your service will suffer.

P.P.S. - The purpose of this love letter was in hopes that I might encourage you to do what I did. Take a moment during this Valentine's season before it end or next season on Valentine's Day and write your service a love letter. She, too, is your partner in life and one who will bring you much joy if you give her some TLC. Because at the end of the day, that love letter is really for you.

9/19/22
Joel P. Brown

PREFACE

Many writers on Amazon don't take the time to see and give back to Amazon for all they have done to provide hope for people, whether in times of unemployment or they simply can't leave the house due to never leaving their home (and that number is according to new research of 2,000 Americans across the country).

To add, people who are severely ill with agoraphobia or COVID-19 might have to stay home longer than 10 days and up to 20 days after symptoms first appeared, but Amazon has made a way for these people to work from home. So, with that in mind I want to give honor to where honor is due and dedicate this stageplay book titled 'The Boy in Amazon's VR CINEPLEX APP' to Amazon as a token of appreciation, by featuring them in it.

But, my reason of being unemployed is not due to a mental illness that prevents me from being in social settings but for defamation.

DEFAMATION: the action of damaging the good reputation of someone; slander or libel.

Defamation is a statement that injures a third party's reputation. The tort of defamation includes both libel (written statements) and slander (spoken statements).

Article 17 of the United Nations International Covenant on Civil and Political Rights states. No one shall be subjected to arbitrary or unlawful interference with his privacy, family, home or correspondence, nor to unlawful attacks on his honour and reputation.

I have not had a solid job since 2013. With that in mind, people have been showing complete hatred towards me an sabotages my efforts at success as what they don't like seeing me do; they report me with false accusations to get me banned on whatever site it is that God seems to be doing something through me.

Jesus, you know how its defamation as no one will not give me a job, or can i find any employment as writing is the only way I have to pay off debt so without any income I have a reason to not pay off debt.

As I have been out of work since 2013 and have not been able to have any kind of solid employment or income to pay bills because of defamation as no one will hire me or give me a job, but God has been faithful to be my source. As I believe God will restore to you the years that the locust hath eaten, the cankerworm, and the caterpiller, and the palmerworm, my great army which I sent among you.

So I want to thank you Kindle Direct Amazon Publishing for allowing writers to become authors from the remote places of their home and make some kind income from it, since I first signed up to join Kindle Direct Amazon Publishing on April 17, 2018 I have published about 67 books; as it has work and live doing what I love most, but see writing as something much more, like a change agent outreach that goes into a readers home under book cover to be of service to that person as an encouragement, through my writing craft while having the ability to inspire change in people.

Writing also serves as a tool to change people's out-look and to give them something to better themselves with as I also get to Connect with People, Walk in their Shoe, and Flip-the-Script to change the scene for a day in hope that it might change the outcome that might be bad to turn it around for the good with a personalized sci-fi short-story.

In attempt to get the person's mind off of a matter that might disturb the comfortable, where I can comfort the disturbed in a created atmosphere of faith that would allow the reader to believe in something more. Nevertheless, to provide good public relations.

With that said, that's why I want to write

because I want to help people put their trust in Christ, by showing the Holy Spirit's beautiful work of "image restoration" in the character that he creates; masterfully remaking a character to more accurately reflect God's virtue. Through sculpting, forming, and transforming a character to better display Christ to the world in a contemporary christian way as the character becomes His image-bearer.

Additionally, publishing on Amazon has helped me to find my cause at heart and that being advocating for missing and exploited children; as it makes me feel like a crime-fighter writer, where I get to come alongside of the NCMEC (National Center for Missing & Exploited Children) to help raise awareness through my literary works to help bring them home.

More about this photo program that I get to be apart of is its called 'Picture them home' — in attempt to help the NCMEC's Photo Partner Program brings together businesses, organizations, employees and the community to help bring missing children home.

Furthermore, Picture Them Home® Campaign has been in operation since 1984 the National Center for Missing & Exploited Children® NCMEC has played an integral role in helping to locate and recover missing children. This is where missing children's posters are one of the tools NCMEC uses to aid the recovery process. These posters bring widespread coverage to missing children's cases and provide NCMEC and indispensable leads. The Picture Them Home Campaign invites businesses and organizations, like mine, to become a part of this effort as Photo Partners.

What does it mean to be a Photo Partner? NCMEC Photo Partners help reunite missing children with their families by displaying or distributing missing children's posters to their employees and the public. Posters featuring more than individual children have since the Picture Them Home Campaign began in 1985. Through the Photo Distribution Program, NCMEC helps ensure companies receive posters in the manner most convenient for them. These posters contain information about missing children and the circumstances surrounding their disappearance. When a child is recovered, Photo and given a replacement photo if needed.

There's a quick rule of thumb that says, *"Don't take for granted science fiction writers. These are people who can destroy yet save entire planets before lunch. Think of what they'll do to for a missing kid to raise awareness and help bring them home."*

One author.
One book.
One kid.
Can change the world.

As stories give hope.

Hope possibilities.
Possibilities freedom.

Be in the moment.

Picture them home with me, and flip a reader's script to help turn their situation around for the good.

It only take one person to bring a missing kid home, and it is possible that that one person could read one of my books and be inspired to return home.

My objective has become to inspire you enough to do a search for the missing kids in your area and to keep them in your mind, if I have done that then I have fulfilled my job.

I love you Amazon, and thanks for reading my emails and being in the moment in my stories. I'm always working on something really special Here.... Can't wait to share. God Bless and keep fighting for missing kids!

Have faith.
Be hopeful.
Stay vigilant.
Keep watch for sightings.
And write them home!

Your zesty movie jumpin' orison throwin' crime-fighting pen-pusher neighborhood friendly,
Joel Flickstein

<u>Prayer for Second chance at life:</u>

Dear father, Just want to say I thank you so much for just being there for me and my family. As you know I have put myself in a horrible situation and I'm just asking for a second chance at life I do not want to leave my family. My life and I have changed so much over the last two years. I am not the same person I was before. I am aware of the sins I committed and I am asking for forgiveness because you are the ultimate judge and decision maker. I do not want to let my children down. If I have not healed from my past please help me I'm asking you I'm begging you. I want to live a better life the right life. Please come to me and help me sacrifice for you o god! Amen!

INTRODUCTION

Character Meet & Greet

Name:
Miles Laverty

Nickname:
The AI cybertronic Robotic Boy, or just Voidboi

Nationality:
Russian/Palestinian

Age:
11-years-old

Birthday:
Feb. 23, 1987

Location:
Star, Kedah

Type:
Human

Occupation:
Student, working in slave labor of child trafficking

Description:
Miles is a spontaneous, energetic and enthusiastic tweenager as life is never boring around him, who has a entertainer of an explorer personality.

The relationship Miles have to other people in the world is a refugee street kid.

Superhero Suit:
The body of the AI cybertronic robotic boy, The Void Boi. The boy's attire looks like a shimmering shiny haptic gaming VR bodysuit made out of 85% Polyester and 15% Spandex fabric that can give you a real feel of the temperature, movement, structure, and texture of different things in and out of virtual reality. It has an AI that gives you intel about his surroundings. It is a lightweight iridescent futuristic virtual reality bodysuit designed in holographic silver dreamy colors that has an eye-catching rainbow effect that changes with light and perspective. It also includes a retractable cloak and a pair of sunglasses. It is a very high-quality VR experience. This suit is very lightweight and comfortable for the players so they can enjoy the virtual environment calmly. This virtual bodysuit has four different kinds of haptic sensations, which can be felt by the players at different levels and environments in the game. Every object has various interactions and sensations with the body of the player in the virtual world.

Superpowers:

Miles' powers are seeing through illusions, super memory, super intelligence, creating phantasm force fields, creating diversions into VR, creating VR illusions and manipulating VR environments, super hearing, and learning the complete history of an object by touching it.

Superhero Weapon:
Glowstick force field saber

Character Narrative: Miles Laverty's Autobiographical Essay

My name is Miles Laverty. I am an eleven year old, who enjoys soccer, swimming, and movies. I am bright and brave, but can also be very sneaky and a bit stingy. I am a Russian and Palestinian Muslim from Star, Kedah. I am currently being home schooled because I have a severe phobia of being in public places, and I am obsessed with the Newsboy style from the 1920s period. Physically, I am in pretty good shape. Although, I am a bit short for my age with pale skin, blonde hair, and blue eyes. I live in a low-class neighborhood. My mother and father are still alive, but live in a third-world country. More about my home schooling is my favourite subjects are maths and science. I love her tutor, Mrs O'Connor but hate my other tutor, Mrs Lee whose interests include looking like a tomato. My best friend is Stephenie. You might say we get on along well, most of the time. I also hang out with Macy and Doyle. They enjoy playing video games together.

Name:
Joel Flickstein

What do other people know them as:
Joel Flickstein calls himself a messenger, and other people know him as a cinephile geek.

Nicknames or 'Also Known As'?
Celluloid

Type:
Human with peculiar powers and abilities

Occupation:
Joel's occupation is a movie projectionist that makes an average $22,200 per year, and $10.67 per hour.

Description:
On Jun 10th, 1954. Joel Flickstein is a Mid-30s year old male figure with brown eyes, underweight, and recognized as a clinical giant. Joel is slightly intelligent and above average with other details that are devout, while he also had a nerdy personality. Nevertheless, Joel's relationship status has been widowed for the past couple of years.

What relationship do they have to other characters in the universe?
Just your friendly Heaven dandy, door opening, Man of Letters, pure flix jumping, prayer intercessory, crime fighter writer superhero with a

mental illness.

Character Narrative: Joel Flickstein's Autobiographical Essay

Joel Flickstein is a Liberal Modern Jewish mid-age man who is set apart from the rest, with a handicap (no arms from the elbows to the hands and no legs from the knees to the feet) that allows him to find creative ways to adapt to anything out of the norm in life. Until one night a dream leads Joel to inherit super-prosthetic limbs (kept inside an iBackPack that attaches to the back of his wheel chair). While if you were to go through Joel Flickstein's closet, you will find that he likes to wear: white collar neon blue polo shirt with white on the hems that are short sleeves and buttons down from 3 buttons in the front. Over this, a 2-inch white tie. Men's fashion khaki cargo shorts with draw strings on the waist band and both sides of the short legs, Joel Flickstein accessorizes his outfit with black retro geek/nerd glasses and a white jewish kippah with a silver star of david displayed on it.

Lastly, he moves around in a Carrier Robotic Wheelchair that basically has a mind of its own like: seat change, over stairs (military style), on the toilet, and standing position to help him to better adapt to life comfortably. Sorry, if it's not that brief as I my imagination started to run wild. If you need anymore info, let me know as I see the iBackPack with the prosthetic limbs inside laying at the foot of the wheel chair.

Carrier Robotic Wheelchair: ROBOTIC WHEELCHAIR WUNKERKIND - Wheelchairs are a dime a dozen but the advent of advance and affordable robotics is truly enabling the disabled. The CARRIER Wheelchair does almost everything – making sure the user is fully independent, capable of traversing any terrain and situation. | vimeo.com/40515866

iBackPack - A bag and gadget cache in one. The basic model has a 10,000mAh battery, 4 USB ports, a retractable power cord, Bluetooth speaker and an anti-theft alarm (via an app). Wi-Fi hotspot and GPS tracking. | youtube.com/watch?v=ub3bqJOzQYY&feature=youtu.be

One night, during the 1950s, while a film projectionist is cleaning and rewarding film reels, in a hot basement of a movie theatre. The cellulose from the celluloid in one film reel overheated to malfunction under a halogen light, causing it to melt and splatter in his eyes as a chemical reaction happened that gave this film projectionist a superhero ability to reenter a movie upon daydreaming to interact with a character for wise guidance. However, he has an audience reading his thoughts that come through like a text message chat on the big screen - without there being a cellphone in his midst - that allows them to see his life being rescripted. Although, he doesn't find this out until he discovers that this movie theater has secrets of its own and has been rescripting his life through every genre to make a movie out of his life for the purpose of saving itself from foreclosure, the world from a corona virus pandemic and the rising of a New World Order. And so, this is the texting story of the movie Journeyer.

Brief Character Study of Joel Flickstein/Celluloid:

It's June 10, 1950s - 3:42 PM ET as Joel Flickstein has come from one of the projectionist booths and he is now in the basement at the ScriptFlipper Theater that's located at 90, Church St., New York, NY 10008-9601; working an overnight shift.

Joel Flickstein wants to get someone to play by his rules because he wants to get a chance at an adventure outside the box, and Joel wants it, now to get someone to rescue him. However, if Joel doesn't get it now; he will allow an anxiety disorder to keep him in a solitary confinement state of mind. While if left untreated it can result in physical deterioration, despair, extreme fear, broken relationships, unemployment, and suicide may be the ultimate outcome.

Therefore Joel Flickstein will get what he wants through a divine intervention that comes through celluloid - to give him the ability to re-enter films - by doing celluloid conception for cognitive treatment that focuses on changing his thoughts and behaviors, as well as establishing new brain interaction patterns.

So in order to get out of the mental and physical box, Joel Flickstein must think inside the box to overcome his anxiety disorder that seems to be keeping him from living an Abundant life of adventure. As the power resides inside the box first as to make any kind of change in your life, you must be able to draw strength and affirmation from inside your own box.

THE BOY IN AMAZON'S VR CINEPLEX APP

A One-Act Play dedicated to Amazon Prime

Characters

THE LAD, 11 – shaggy hair. Caucasian. He often wears a beat-up 1920s style Newsboy cap with Newsie shirt, button fronts vest, hook & loop fastener side closure flat front with gathered elastic waist in back pants, suspenders that have button holes to attach to buttons on pants waistband, and shabby Edwardian Newsboy boots. He used to be very into Jazz.

JOEL FLICKSTEIN/CELLULOID, 35 – 1950s ducktail haircut with sides and back of the hair combed towards the center to create what strongly resembles a duck's tail. Mixed African-American and Caucasian. Bespectacled. He wears a 1950s button fronts halfway buttoned collar dress shirt with sleeves rolled up to elbows, suspenders that have clamps to attach to pants waistbands, and trousers with two pleats cuffed two and a half inches at the knee. He doesn't wear shoes because he is crippled from the hands to elbows and feet to knees and gets around in a wheelchair, but when he has time-traveled to a period in the future in his superhero suit of CELLULOID his arms and legs are restored and fully-functional. In love with the movies.

Setting:

A modern day movie theater in virtual reality. The set is the raked movie theater audience, ten to fifteen of black seats with a dingy carpeted aisle guided by walk way lights running up the sides. The upstage wall is the back wall of the movie theater, with a window into the projection booth. There is a metal door leading out into the hallway to the movie theater lobby that gives the impression as if it was a real movie theater. We, the theater audience are the movie screen. The beam of light from the projector radiates out over our heads. A mysterious 11-year-old moviegoer boy sits in this darkened movie theater alone.

Time:

Summer, occurring in a Utopia city during a time period in the Thirtieth Century of the year 3020, when smartphones are much more than phones and are far more advanced.

PRE-SHOW

After the theater audience has filed in, the house lights slowly dim (onstage in the virtual movie theater audience and also in the theater audience) to a darkened theater, a spotlight shines center stage on a human cryopresavation taking place of the process of chilling a human body to extremely low temperatures, happening in a fluorescent glowy transparent cryopresavation human case that looks like a block of ice as fog surrounds it. Inside this cryopreservation case, the figure of an adolescent is seen with some kind of device on his head as a cross set of wires that's jumbled together run from the headset through the block of ice to disappear off stage. A strobe light flashes for a couple of seconds before all lights black out to leave the theater in total darkness.

George A. Johnson's original titled Trailer to "Pulled from Darkness" (the real life story of a Ukrainian woman who was separated from her three children and sold into trafficking by Russian gangsters. Defying all odds, she survived to be reunited with her children.) starts playing, and the light from the projector beams out over our heads. Images that we cannot decipher are being projected. Dust motes are illuminated by the light.

This last 2 minutes or so (from beginning to end of the soundtrack of 'Sleepy Little Eyes' from the movie) and all we can see are abstracted dancing images shooting out of the film projector.

Then the soundtrack ends, and the unknown movie ends, and there is a bright flash of green, and then white, and then the sound of the film reaching the end of its spool in the projector. The virtual movie theater lights automatically flicker on, the lad slides down in his front row seat, and after about 5 seconds...

Blackout:

ACT ONE

SCENE ONE

Lights up:

(A lad sits in the front row aisle seat of the virtual movie theater, pondering to himself a superhero that he has heard about as if he was speaking out loud.)

THE LAD.

He was just a crippled cinephile who found creative ways to adjust to his present limitations at work as a projectionist for a second-run movie theater empowered by a Supreme-Being with supernatural intuition, insight, visionary powers and time-travel movie jumping into the future; but he has yet to find out that the site at the 4-Star Theatre is sacred to a Supreme Being changes the course of his destiny every time he impulsively decide to jump into future movies before the eyes of moviegoers who watch as his life is projected on the big screen through flixtexting stories. Until one day, your not-so-average joe flickstein drops into virtual reality to watch a movie and to be swept away by the sunny-natured characters, that would make me forget about his stresses for a while. It was farewell to all the worries and cares of the day. It was time instead to unwind and dream a little in the midst of times that tried men's souls, when the glitz and glamour of Hollywood kept the moviegoers distracted and entertained. I retained a fresh new perspective, and most valuably, allowed me to hold on, to my national sense of humor.

Blackout:

SCENE TWO

Lights up:

(Joel Flickstein as CELLULOID pops into a centered seat in this Amazon Prime VR Movie Theater. He is completely oblivious of the lad who sits silently motionless in the front row aisle seat, while from behind you can barely make out the tip of his Newsboy cap in this dimly lit virtual theater. Simultaneously, Joel Flickstein's conscious comes into play and speaks his thoughts as if they were recording his experience on the pages of a journal.)

JOEL FLICKSTEIN.
Cold was the night. The night was young. The moon was full. The lights have dimmed to black.

I'm situated in a digital black theater single recliner in VR. There's no one in Amazon's Prime Video VR App a stirring, it's just me, experiencing a Prime Video in my own virtual theater as this movie plays, or... so I think. Then, from out of the blue, a young lad appeared in the aisle seat on the second roll. I thought to my self... What that person doing in here? No one's supposed to be in here but me, as I wondered if it was some kind of glitch in the app that intertwined someone else's VR prime movie experience with mine. So I went on watching my movie, and while watching this unexpected stranger from out of my peripheral vision; as he never moved, until the movie was over; he blipped out.

Blackout:

Lights up:

(The next day, Joel Flickstein as CELLULOID pops into a centered seat in this Amazon Prime VR Movie Theater. He is aware of the lad who sits silently motionless in the front row aisle seat, while from behind you can barely make out the tip of his Newsboy cap in this dimly lit virtual theater. Simultaneously, Joel Flickstein's conscious comes into play and speaks his thoughts as if they were recording his experience on the pages of a journal.)

JOEL FLICKSTEIN.

This time when I entered my VR theater. I found the same young lad there before me situated in the same seat, but one row closer to me; as he sat again without any motion, just starring off into the big screen. I thought about saying something to the kid, but how would he if I'm not able to speak in this particular app? So I did the next best thing and reported him to Amazon within my VR prime movie experience, and after that kept watching the movie before me as I kept an eye on the kid from my peripheral vision.

Blackout:

Lights up:

(Day three, Joel Flickstein as CELLULOID pops into a centered seat in this Amazon Prime VR Movie Theater. He is aware of the lad who sits silently motionless in the front row aisle seat, while from behind you can barely make out the tip of his Newsboy cap in this dimly lit virtual theater. Simultaneously, Joel Flickstein's conscious comes into play and speaks his thoughts as if they were recording his experience on the pages of a journal.)

JOEL FLICKSTEIN.
I go to watch a movie again, and there the same lad is, sitting in the same aisle sit but a row closer to me. At this point I'm getting a little freaked out because who ever he is he's not supposed to be in

this VR app with me, according Amazon's response to the report I made on him; as they told me that I wasn't alone, not long after a man purchased an Oculus and downloaded the Prime Video app he began to experience strange happenings, too, like what I described. I was also told that a person named Miles Laverty and he had been haunting the Amazon Prime VR Movie theater, and that people kept seeing him as an avatar. Another person reported a claim of having heard laughter, like a giggle, but in VR you only can hear and speak unless the app allows it. Then, Miles came into the possession of a mixed reality, the Sega VR headset in 1991. This multi-pod Virtuality system was once owned by a Electronic Visualization Lab rat of the infamous serial killer, a man who had preyed upon young gamers while dressed as his "alter-ego" avatar, a boy named Glitch. When Miles was on human trials, he watched movie, and some of these disturbing movie were kept in the Sega VR headset. People who have entered their own prime movie theater have experienced bizarre happenings, as Amazon support advised that I keep an eye out for the kid so I did just that from my peripheral vision while continuing to watch the movie. But for some reason I couldn't believe that was the whole story.

Blackout:

Lights up:

(Day four, Joel Flickstein as CELLULOID pops into a centered seat in this Amazon Prime VR Movie Theater. He is aware of the lad who sits silently motionless in the front row aisle seat, while from behind you can barely make out the tip of his Newsboy cap in this dimly lit virtual theater. Simultaneously, Joel Flickstein's conscious comes into play and speaks his thoughts as if they were recording his experience on the pages of a journal.)

JOEL FLICKSTEIN.

The next day, I found myself returning to my prime VR movie theater as usual, not to sit through a flick, but more of as a pursuit wanting to kill the cat from the curiosity that kept it in the questioning mind of a rug rat. Only to notice that the lad had jumped a seat from the aisle, and was now sitting three sits away from me. What else was I supposed to do but act like I was watching the movie while observing the kid from my peripheral vision?

Blackout:

Lights up:

(Day five, Joel Flickstein as CELLULOID pops into a centered seat in this Amazon Prime VR Movie Theater. He is aware of the lad who sits silently motionless in the front row aisle seat, while from behind you can barely make out the tip of his Newsboy cap in this dimly lit virtual theater. Simultaneously, Joel Flickstein's conscious comes into play and speaks his thoughts as

if they were recording his experience on the pages of a journal.)

JOEL FLICKSTEIN.

The following day, after I have put on my VR headset and entered my prime screening room to study this figment of the app more, creepier things began to happen as the lad had jumped seats; he was now sitting two seats away from me in the same aisle that was in front of me. My eyes glanced on the screen and back on the lad as I motioned my index finger outside of VR to squeeze the trigger on the controller to turn the lights on in the VR screening room, and when I did just that, the lad blipped out and into the next seat in sync with the lights as they gradually turned on and off; he was now one seat away from me. I didn't know what else to do but remove my headset to prevent the unthinkable from happening.

Blackout:

Lights up:

(Day six, Joel Flickstein as CELLULOID pops into a centered seat in this Amazon Prime VR Movie Theater. He is aware of the lad who sits silently motionless in the front row aisle seat, while from behind you can barely make out the tip of his Newsboy cap in this dimly lit virtual theater. Simultaneously, Joel Flickstein's

conscious comes into play and speaks his thoughts as if they were recording his experience on the pages of a journal.)

JOEL FLICKSTEIN.
I was so shaken out of my skin after what I've experienced with this lad, that I didn't go back into Amazon's Prime Video app, until two days after yesterday, and this time when I dropped into my VR screening room the lad was sitting right in front of me. But, before I could imagine any preconceived notions I casted off my VR headset, and I don't know when I'm going to put it on again.

Blackout:

Lights up:

(Day seven, Joel Flickstein as CELLULOID pops into a centered seat in this Amazon Prime VR Movie Theater. He is aware of the lad who sits silently motionless in the front row aisle seat, while from behind you can barely make out the tip of his Newsboy cap in this dimly lit virtual theater. Simultaneously, Joel Flickstein's conscious comes into play and speaks his thoughts as if they were recording his experience on the pages of a journal.)

JOEL FLICKSTEIN.
About a week later, the suspense this lad had created was killing me and I couldn't resist finding out what could be so I put my headset on and

entered the VR screening room once again. Only thing is... Once inside... the lad was no where to be found, until I turned my head to find him in the seat next to me. Then, following this he pointed towards the screen where my eyes shifted and what comes next changed my whole impressions on the lad; as he projected his thoughts of what he had to say in captions on the screen, as they played out through the movie.

(George A. Johnson's prelude to "Sleepy Little Eyes" starts playing, and the light from the projector beams out over our heads. Images that we cannot decipher are being projected. Dust motes are illuminated by the light. This last for the duration of the lad's monologue or so (from beginning to end of the soundtrack of 'Little Sleepy Eyes') and all we can see are abstracted dancing images shooting out of the film projector.

(Simultaneously, the lad's conscious comes into play, and he projects his thoughts through the movie that tells his story through the sound system.)

THE LAD.

I'm sorry to freak you out, as no one has ever stayed after seeing me move pass the second seat, but thanks for baring with me. Have you ever heard of cryonics is the low temperature preservation of a human corpse, with the hope that resuscitation and restoration to life and full health may be possible in the future. Cryopreservation of humans is not reversible with present technology, and use cryoprotectants to prevent ice formation during cryopreservation. Cryonicists hope that medical advances will someday allow cryopreserved bodies to be revived. It is not known if it will ever be possible to revive a cryopreserved human cadaver. In other words, cryonics is another fancy way for a person to say, "frozen in time." Likewise, have you ever been in a coma? Just shake you head as I know how you can't speak in here. Its interesting how a coma is defined as a state of unconsciousness, and which a person is unaware of what's going on around them most comas last for a few days... but in rare cases they can last for years... but the brain continuing to show some electrical activity... and that electrical activity mean that the person in the coma is still thinking... as they are able to hear in the coma and even see people. Currently, I am experiencing both of being frozen in time and in a coma. I've been in this coma for almost 6 years, as no nobody has been able to communicate with me, or even see me outside of this app. Even though I'm still breathing on my own and there's still some brain activity, but unfortunately after all this time it doesn't necessarily indicate a conscious, as the EEG are monitoring my brain activity more closely with a new EG machine as we speak. This doesn't affect me physically, and I'm thankful they've installed a network, so their computer system can be hooked up to the internet because, if it wasn't for someone having had been very sloppy with the installation all of this wouldn't be possible. As some kind of overload or short needs in that wire, that somehow made the EEG wires shorted to the Ethernet wires, that made a way for me to send my conscience out directly from my brain onto the internet, that transferred it into an avatar to gave me an escape from out of my captivity, and into this place in virtual reality. And what happened was a one in a zillion chance, and by divine intervention that'll never happen again. That's how I ended up in here, as I'd rather be stuck in a utopia-type of refuge, than stuck in a place of painful oppression. You know what they say, one window into an oppressor's programming is through their communication. How do they talk about the people they oppress and work with? And here's how I ended up being frozen in time in a coma...It all started when I persuaded one of my kidnappers with my inventor skills just enough to get him to entrust me as his prisoner to recreate one of those Google Cardboard Topmaxions 3D Virtual Reality DIY VR Headsets for Movies and Games, that are compatible with Andriod and Apple that's up to 6 inches easy setup machines for him; and it totally backfired, but backlashed for me, he's how I got to the place I am now. It all started with I was captured in 2019. After five years of captivity, I began losing hope of ever getting home. Then, one of my kidnappers who have grown fawning adoration on me was having trouble setting up his new mobile device and I wooed him to ask me for help. It turned out that I was able to convince him to let me show him how I can build a Google Cardboard

Topmaxions 3D Virtual Reality DIY VR Headset, that I bluffed would be untrackable and used for movies and games. Then I gain his confidence to get an Internet connection after it was built, which I then used to make another way of escape through VR, but have been unable to tell anyone of my location because in the Amazon Prime VR experience, you can't talk. Of course I was able to free my mind in VR, but I'm still held captive in the world as I now had been comatose for seven months and frozen in time with the the 3D VR headset I've made on me, by the very person I gained trust with who seemed to have slipped through the cracks, when his Pizza-Related Pedophile Ring were captured in Afghanistan. I guess its his way of showing affection towards me by still giving my a way of escape through virtual reality, but my twitterpated captor doesn't know I found away to make contact with the one superhero who I know can save me - You, CELLULOID. I know this is a safe place to share and my secret's safe with you, but if its alright with you I'd like to tell you what they did in there. I was one of those victims who stayed silent for a while. They paid my family $5,000 to get us out of hardships, according to an agreement made by my parents to be sold into indentured servitude to pay-off the debt. As I'm from Vladivostok, Russia but grew up in Langkawi, Kedah, Malaysia, yet I've always wanted to live and work in the United States just not like this. When a recruiter proposed an opening at a hotel, my parents happily signed me over in exchange... for the payment of $5,000 to get us out of our hardships and for the opportunity for me to travel to the US and live out my dream. When I got there, I quickly discovered that the job opportunity was a farce. I was bused to a Gulf State against my will, that was a three-day journey without food or water. Once at my destination, I was forced to work 18-hour days cleaning hotels for a pittance. Concerned that the recruiter would retaliate against my family back in Langkawi, Malaysia for the initial debt, I did what they told me. As a child in this hotel of horror, I was raped, abused and sold to men who employed me for sex. The brutality ended when I was 12, and built that 3D VR headset for that one twitterpated captiver. But, like many boy victims, I didn't seek help, or didn't tell anyone about the trauma I had suffered until now. Instead, I buried my pain and shame deep inside, carrying the burden alone and in silence until now. Silence did not equal acceptance, and I'm lucky because I shouldn't be here. I put a lot of focus and energy into taking my own life, as two suicide attempts failed. And I was preparing for a third attempt when my intervention came in the form of an idea to befriend the one captor, who was twitterpated over me, and build the 3D VR headset. So I decided to obey that prompting and finally to reach out for help through that device. Even then, years after the exploitation ended in my mind, my tortuous journey for my body hasn't because I'm still frozen in time. So, will you help me, by finding my body in the time I'm living in and free me from this captivity once and for all?

(Then the soundtrack ends, and the movie that the lad had projected himself into ends, and there is a bright flash of green, and then white, and then the sound of the film reaching the end of its spool in the projector as the lad appears seated in his front aisle row seat.)

[Sorrowfully, Joel nods in agreement with the lad as a tear streams down the side of his cheek.]

(Simultaneously, Joel Flickstein's conscious comes into play and speaks his thoughts as if they were recording his experience on the pages of a journal.)

JOEL.
While the lad was talking, it appears that Amazon Prime had updated their app with a flixtexting feature, that allows me to cross-communicate with other users in the app through text-to-speech, and this is what I said after I've discovering it... Without a shadow of doubt, I agreed to do just that and more that he didn't asked for; I told the lad this is how its going down... I will not only save your life but also your mind and spirit, by giving you the gift of an immortal union, through an artificial intelligence cybertronics body that will allow you to be a robot boy in the real world that you can enter through your avatar for the time being. Promptly, after downloading your conscience in the programming of this robotic boy; for you, this

artificial intelligence state of art will not only re-create your human body, but it will create your immortality. One of the most powerful messages in this epic that this will send, will be a tribute to inner freedom, immortal love, and the inexorable right to honor one's truth. It will be a beautiful event, thing or person in the natural instinctive state of mind deriving from one's situation, mood, or relationships with others is immortalized in the work of art, seen through the eyes of the artist that alludes to the passion or a zealous intensity of the experience that will stay with the spectator a long time. The artist's art captures a lifetime of emotion or mood that will even survive after death. For the spectator, the art will not only create a masterpiece - it will create the artist's immortality, also. I'll get on it right away, and download your conscience into the robotic boy pronto once done, before setting out to the location of your human body to relieve it from out of captivity and bring your twitterpated captor to justice. Well, that's all for now, see you soon.

Blackout:

SCENE THREE

Lights up:

(Simultaneously, the lad's conscious comes into play and speaks his thoughts as if they were recording his experience on the pages of a journal.)

(Setting: A mysterious moviegoer sits in a darkened movie theater with his back towards us, and as the projector flickers a beam of light overhead that projects a title screen on the screen before the man, a dim light shines upon his face, revealing that it has been the lad, Miles Laverty, who has been telling the story all along.)

THE LAD.

THREE MONTHS passed. The seasons came and went, the short animal lives fled by. A time came when there was no one who remembered the name of Miles Laverty, except for the old days before his abduction. But the dawn of a new name has come, The Void Boi, that would leave a lasting legacy as Joel Flickstein has brought forth the body of the AI cybertronic robotic boy. The boy's attire looks like a shimmering shiny haptic gaming VR bodysuit made out of 85% Polyester and 15% Spandex fabric that can give you a real feel of temperature, movement, structure, and texture of different things in and out of virtual reality. It has an AI that gives you intel about his surroundings. It is a lightweight iridescent futuristic virtual reality bodysuit designed in holographic silver dreamy colors that has an eye-catching rainbow effect that changes with light and perspective. It also includes a retractable cloak and a pair of sunglasses. It is a very high-quality VR experience. This suit is very lightweight and comfortable for the players so they can enjoy the virtual environment calmly. This virtual bodysuit has four different kinds of haptic sensations, which can be felt by the players at different levels and environments in the game. Every object has various interactions and sensations with the body of the player in the virtual world. And now it was time for Joel Flicktein as CELLULOID to bring the Twitterpated Captor to justice, who was an old man with a growth disorder when found, cradling in his arms Miles Laverty as Miles was nothing more than just a brain in a jar from the 1997 period, who had tricked Joel into making the remnants of this boy into a superhero; so he could live again for an ulterior motive as an opportunistic sexual liaison with the Twitterpated Captor. But, since a mind is a terrible thing to waste and the download of Mile's conscience has already been complete in the AI cybertronic robotic boy body, Joel initiated Miles into his FilMilitiamen secret revolutionary organization and adopted him as his very own son, where he would be kept safe. And as for the old Twitterpated Captor with a growth disorder, he was captured and sentenced to 40 years in federal prison for sex trafficking minor boys and for carrying out a year-long scheme with his other confidantes to groom and sexually abuse underage boys. As key informants pointed out their belief that law enforcement has very little understanding of (commercially exploited) boys, as when filing human the trafficking report, they asked: 'Why couldn't he get away? He's a boy.' One informant said he was forced to explain to law enforcement professionals before filing a report that boys and young men can be bought and sold just like girls. The Twitterpated Captor did not testify in his defense during the trial late year, which ended with his conviction on five counts, including sex trafficking of a minor. But on a Wednesday he spoke in court to the victims shortly before the sentence was handed down.

Blackout:

THE END!

CAST/CHARACTER

Miles Laverty as The Lad

Miles is an 11-year-old mixed raced Russian/
Palestinian boy from Star, Kedah, who
enjoys soccer and swimming.

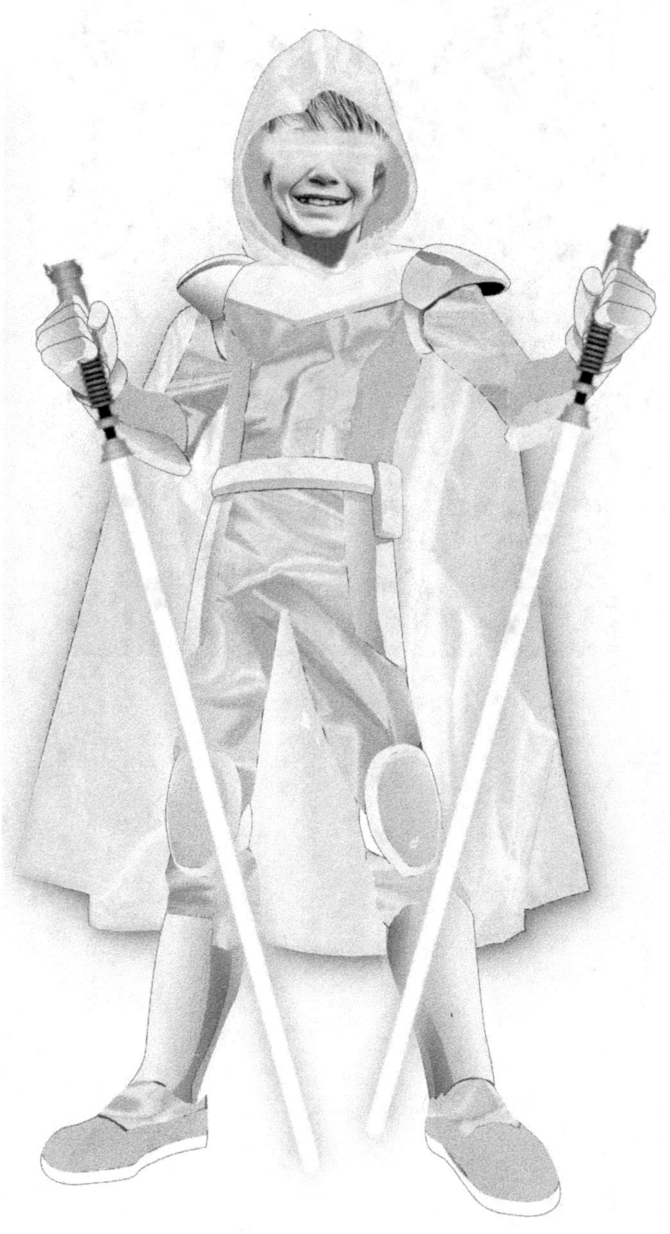

FUN ARCHAIC WORDS GLOSSARY

You won't find these archaic words in most dictionaries that you've encountered through the story, but take my word for – they're real and just for fun as they can show that you don't have to cuss in a book to make it good.

1. HOBBERDEHOY – A youth entering manhood
2. FAFFLE – To stutter or mumble
3. DASYPYGAL – Having a hairy buttocks
4. CORNOBBLED – Hit with a fish
5. COLLIESHANGIE – A noisy or confused fight
6. WEM – A stain, flaw, or scar
7. CALCOGRAPHER – One who draws with chalk
8. BODEWASH – Cow dung
9. TWIDDLEPOOP – An effeminate looking man
10. LIRIPOOP – A silly creature
11. LEPTORRHINIAN – Having long narrow

nose

12. BRIDELOPE – When the new bride is "both symbolically and physically swept off on horse-back" to the husband's home
13. MUNDUNGUS – Garage; stinky tobacco
14. CHIROGYMNAST – A finger-exercise machine for pianists
15. TOXOPHILLY – love of archery
16. PISMIRE – An ant
17. VALGUS – Bowlegged or knock-kneed
18. XYSTUS – An indoor porch for exercising
19. winter
20. LUMENTOUS – Having a strong animal smell
21. SAPROSTOMOUS – Having bad breath
22. BALBRIGGAN – A fine cotton used mainly for underwear.
23. ATMATERTERA – A great-grandfather's grand-mother's sister
24. ANISOGNATHOUS – Having the upper and lower teeth unlike
25. WHIPJACK - Beggar pretending to have been shipwrecked
26. SPODOGENOUS – Pertaining to or due to the presence of waste matter
27. CRAPANDINA – A mineral such as toadstone or bufonite said to have healing properties
28. GALLIGASKIN – Baggy trousers

AFTERWORD

THE REDEEMER
a monologue by Cybele May

Stewart, a detective driven to the edge, returns from a failed attempt to retrieve a kidnapped boy, and makes an unusual confession.

STEWART.

It was an accident. *(Pause)* We were in the car. We were running late. She was supposed to have hemmed the pants of my suit. She hadn't only I didn't know until I put 'em on so I had to keep them up with masking tape. It looked terrible but she kept saying that we were going to be late. So we were in the car and she looked down at me and said I looked ridiculous and she was glad that she had no standards left otherwise she would be humiliated to be seen with me. That's when I started yelling— what did she want from me? She wanted me to lose control, didn't she? And then she started laughing. The faster I drove the funnier I was and the louder she laughed. I couldn't take it, I couldn't take any of it anymore. We were ugly. I wanted both of us dead. Suddenly, I wanted it all to be over and I turned straight into the oncoming traffic. *(Pause)* I forgot Tommy was in the back. I forgot my boy was there. He was dressed up in his little blue suit. If it hadn't been so messed up in the accident he would have been buried in it. He was so quiet, quiet all the time. Shiny black hair, brown eyes. He had freckles from playing soccer all summer with the neighbor kid in the yard. He'd curl up on my lap and put his face against my chest and tap along with my heart. We used to eat cereal for supper when his mother wasn't home. *(Pause)* I told everyone it was my fault. They'd just hug me and say it would be okay and that I'd stop blaming myself someday. They didn't realize that I had actually done it, it really was my fault.

Like what that monologue portrayed, most boys are silenced when they are going through a tragedy to the point that the shock of it paralyzes them from wanting to scream.

Boys — the silent victims of sex trafficking

"More than 1 million children, according to the International Labour Organization, are exploited each year in the commercial sex trade. IndyStar columnist Tim Swarens, through the support of a Society of Professional Journalists fellowship, spent more than a year investigating a lucrative business where children are abused with low risk to buyers or traffickers, despite tougher laws and heightened international awareness of the scourge. Google, Eli Lilly and Co.,

and Indiana Wesleyan University provided additional support for this project." — Tim Swarens, IndyStar

As a child, Tom Jones was raped, abused and sold to men for sex. The brutality ended when he was 15. But, like many male victims, Jones didn't seek help, didn't tell anyone about the trauma he had suffered. Instead, he buried his pain and shame deep inside, carrying the burden alone and in silence for another 15 years. Silence did not equal acceptance. "I'm lucky, because I shouldn't be here," Jones says. "I put a lot of focus and energy into taking my own life." Two suicide attempts failed. And Jones says he was preparing for a third attempt when he decided finally to reach out for help. Even then, years after the exploitation ended, it was difficult for Jones to acknowledge what he had suffered. "I was very ashamed to talk to a therapist who I knew cared about me," he says. Key informants pointed out their belief that law enforcement has very little understanding of (commercially exploited) boys. For example, when filing human trafficking reports, they would often ask: 'Why couldn't he get away? He's a boy.' One informant said she was forced to explain to law enforcement professionals before filing a report that boys and young men can be bought and sold just like girls. And Boys Too. Boys hear that it only happens to girls, but this is seen as a gender-biased, gender-specific issue. The fight against trafficking in the U.S. delivered the same message. Boys, they told me, are rarely the victims of commercial exploitation. The UN and others are not acknowledging the problem. They're just not getting it in terms of the sex trafficking of males. It makes me very angry that boys are exploited far more often than is commonly understood.

"In 2016, a Department of Justice-commissioned study, Youth Involvement in the Sex Trade, found that boys make up about 36% of children caught up in the U.S. sex industry (about 60% are female and less than 5% are transgender males and females)."

"In 2008, researchers from the John Jay School of Criminal Justice reported that boys account for about 45% of child trafficking victims in New York City."

"When you wake up to it, when you see how big it is," Jones says, "I don't know how you turn away."

Wake up! Boy's manhood is under attack!

"Sexual assault can happen to anyone, no matter your age, sexual orientation, or gender identity. Men and boys who have been sexually assaulted or abused may have many of the same feelings and reactions as other survivors of sexual assault, but they may also face some additional challenges because of social attitudes and stereotypes about men and masculinity." - rainn.org

"Men and boys who have been sexually assaulted may experience the same effects of sexual assault as

other survivors, and they may face other challenges that are more unique to their experience." - rainn.org

"Some men who have survived sexual assault as adults feel shame or self-doubt, believing that they should have been "strong enough" to fight off the perpetrator. Many men who experienced an erection or ejaculation during the assault may be confused and wonder what this means. These normal physiological responses do not in any way imply that you wanted, invited, or enjoyed the assault. If something happened to you, know that it is not your fault and you are not alone." - rainn.org

"Men who were sexually abused as boys or teens may also respond differently than men who were sexually assaulted as adults." - rainn.org

Even though sexual abuse or assualt tends to cause an identity crisis and cause a boy to question their manhood with survivors, this happens within every boy, whether with or without a father present in the home.

"Sexual assault is in no way related to the sexual orientation of the perpetrator or the survivor, and a person's sexual orientation cannot be caused by sexual abuse or assault. Some men and boys have questions about their sexuality after surviving an assault or abuse—and that's understandable. This can be especially true if you experienced an erection

or ejaculation during the assault. Physiological responses like an erection are involuntary, meaning you have no control over them." - rainn.org

Sometimes perpetrators, especially adults who sexually abuse boys, will use these physiological responses to maintain secrecy by using phrases such as, "You know you liked it." If you have been sexually abused or assaulted, it is not your fault. In no way does an erection invite unwanted sexual activity, and ejaculation in no way condones an assault." - rainn.org

5 Attacks on the Souls of Men that puts Manhood Under Spiritual Attack:

1. Manhood Under Attack: PRIDE

2. Manhood Under Attack: IDENTITY

3. Manhood Under Attack: PASSIVITY

4. Manhood Under Attack: ISOLATION

5. Manhood Under Attack: LUST

Male sexuality is under assault.

Prong of the attack against masculinity is a social one. Being manly has in many ways become "politically incorrect." Men are encouraged to be sensitive and feeling and suppress their natural characteristics to be aggressive and tough.

Becoming a man is not simply a function of going through puberty. Becoming a man has traditionally been seen as the transition from having the values and attitudes of a boy to acquiring the values and attitudes that we instinctively recognize as manly. This transition requires healthy masculine role models who can guide boys through the rites of passage that turn them into men. Most men in modern society have not had healthy male rites of passage.

Guys, it's time to defend our right to be men.

Unfortunately, many of the popular movies, TV and literature of today do not provide very healthy examples of mature masculinity. In fact, you'll often find men portrayed as grown-up, irresponsible boys.

Since that time, I've noticed how often this happens in modern movies and TV shows. Instead of being shown as respectable leaders who are willing to set aside their own comfort to do their duty with courage, it has become popular to portray men as weaker than women and less capable. It's not that women aren't better at certain things than men, it's just that the idea that men have suppressed women for generations has become so entrenched in the popular mind set that male bashing has begun to be accepted as "normal."

In spite of that, society might believe that *"The definition of manhood above has been my goal as a dad: help my son reach a level of maturity to embrace and enjoy this sense of masculine responsibility. A boy becomes a man when he becomes*

*mature enough to embrace and enjoy the sense
of responsibility to lead, provide for, and protect
women and children in ways appropriate to a man's
differing relationships in order to fulfill humanity's
God-given commission." - desiringgod.org*

*"The concept of manhood is relatively new to some.
Perhaps because some grew up without the consistent
influence of any man, as some aren't aware that there is
a unique identity that only men could feel. Some men
know they they are stronger, in general, and their lies
come more to the surface, but other than this, they don't
know the distinctions. The feeling of manhood is short-
lived. There is such an thing as a real man, a God's man,
a man's man, but since some hadn't kept any of the
promises, a growing doubt is seeded that some might
not be the real thing. Some don't know exactly what a
man is. Some have been taught what a man does and
how loud a man must cheer, but apart from the 'Real
Men Love Jesus' shallow bumper-sticker logic that's
floating around there, that doesn't define the terms
which makes some men find themselves looking for a
general definition. Because, if they had a general
definition of a man, they would know whether or not
they were one. Some boys seek out a men's gathering,
where they talk and do manly things and continue to
wonder is they were one of the guys, wondering if they
were really a man. Doing manly things doesn't make
you more of a man than clothes do not make the man,
the saddle does not make the horse, or what is outside
yourself does not convey much worth. And so for a long*

time some wondered around the in a fog about their manhood, feeling like manhood is like something that had been handed to them accidentally. Some men begin to wonder, if there wasn't some kind of male spirit God put in a man that was more general. In a guy there is something else, more like the spirit of a tractor or a calculator. And moreover, they wonder how that spirit was confirmed, how a person knew he had it. The idea that manhood is passed down from father to son has been an unpleasant thought. We all carry a 'father wound,' and unless our father convinces us we have what it takes, we are probably going to flounder for a while. God wants to heal the father wound, and how our identity as men comes from Him, how He steps in when our fathers step out. What I want to talk about, though, is how I got the knowing without getting it from my father. The thing I believe about manhood now is that it lives within the male from a very early age, and sometimes it gets awakened, and sometimes it doesn't. It doesn't matter how old you are - a man is a man is a man. How would you define a real man? You might say, a real man is somebody who provides for his family. That is something a 'good' man does, but I don't think you have to do that to be a (real) man. Or, you might say, a real man is honest, he doesn't lie. That is a very good answer, but again, this is something a good man does, but not a qualifier for what makes a man a man. Or, you might say that a real man drives a truck! Not a qualifier I am looking for, as it's obvious that none of these are the right answers. So, take out a sheet a paper, because I am going to give you the definition of a real man. And you are going to come back to this over the next several years, because there are going to be times when you will wonder whether you are a real man, and have here is a sure way to find out. Let me give you God's definition of a real man. I have searched through the Bible, and I have thought a great deal about it. If you have this thing, then, according to God, you are a real man. God's definition of a real man . . . is . . . a person . . . , with . . ., the ultimate qualifier of a man, the sure sign that God is heaven had spoken, that God in His infinite wisdom and perfection had endorsed them as men . . . a person with . . . a penis! If you have a penis, God has spoken. Whatever it is God puts in a man has been in all of us since we were young, and how the wealth of our country has caused something called 'suspended adolescence,' so that some of us haven't stepped into the truth that we are men - instead we are still living like children. YOU ARE A MAN, BOYS AND MAN! You are men. Some of you have never heard this before, but i want to tell you, you are men. You are not boys, you are not children, you are not women, you are men. God has spoken, and when God speaks, you are, the majority has spoken. You are men. There's no telling what kind of messages boy are getting about who they really were (especially after the violation of rape or molestation that is happening to boys that make them go silent). The hard truth is, though, just because God made us men doesn't mean we are done. I know the journey of a man is difficult, and that, there are forces that are always against us. Elaborating on how to navigate the journey of manhood is not something I know more about than these guys, but I think it bears repeating that, if God has spoken, the journey belongs to you and me as much as it belongs to a man who grew up with a father. And it's a journey we are on whether we like it or not. If you begin to doubt your manhood, if you doubt you have what it takes, you simply have to duck into the nearest bathroom and check you shorts. If God has spoken, then you have within you whatever it takes to do the things a man needs to do, to become a good man for a woman, for some kids, for an office, for whatever it is God wants you to do." - Paraphrased from Donald Miller's book, 'To Own a Dragon: Reflections of growing up without a Father,' Chapter 7 - Manhood: The Right Equiptment

Boys are made to believe that you have to be something much more to be a man, when really its as simple as knowing you have something between your legs.

So, don't act like a man too young, enjoy your childhood while you have it because you only get one.

I know when you scream in the darkness of your soul,

no one hears you,

you scream for someone to help,

no one hears you,

you cry and tear youself apart

but still no one hears you

no one cares you may feel

no one wants to help

so you shut your self in,

so no one hears you,

you close yourself from everyone

so no one hears you, you feel,

no one cares, you think,

no one wants to help, it seems.

But, pain is a microphone

and the more it hurts,

the louder you get.

Suffering isn't an obstacle to being used by God.

It is an opportunity to be used like never before.

The Lord is near to the brokenhearted.

So, raise your voice!

And be the voice that echoes for the voiceless!

Just don't stay speechless or silent!

Adam's story:

*"Do not internalize the abuse, because
that will make it seem that the abuse
is happening all over again."*

Brad's story:

*"I think for me and possibly other men, it's a
huge pride thing—feeling like you have to be the
man and face your problems and get over it."*

Brian's story:

*"Showing emotion about being abused? It's not
well-accepted. As a Black man, you've been broken
down so much that you have to put on a face of being
strong. We have a lot of pain that is unattended to."*

Danyol's story:

*"Talking about it really does take
back power from the trauma."*

Keith's story:

*"I was afraid of what people would think.
I was ashamed that a man sexually assaulted
me...that I didn't fight hard enough."*

AN INVITATION OF HOPE

"The Lord is my director; I have no objective or no need to use the Stanislavsky method or Meisner technique. He makes me to recline back in cozy theaters; He shows me pleasant motion pictures. He blows my mind; He sends me on a journey of adventure for all His glory. Yaaas, though I'm blocked through scenes of horrible darkness, I'll fear no evil; for You make a cameo with me and steal the show; Your props and Your set, they comfort me. You provide a crafts service for me 25/7 in front of my critics; You capture my best headshot with grace and no Photoshop; my thirst is quenched, because there is unlimited refills. Expecting popcorn, raisin nets, sprite (goodness), discounts and bonuses (mercy) to follow me. Throughout the calendar of my life; and I will rest with my eyes open in the theater of my director for all eternity." - Joel Brown's personal version of Psalm 23

"God is my director and I'm just His actor, with the Bible He gives me as my script. So I learn my lines for Him to block out my cues on the stage of the world that's

in His hands, walking out His words that I put what was learned into practice to make His script come alive. While living them out on this stage He sets for me to shine His message for His glory, that's told through my vocation with each scene being like a new episode on a TV show. Where in-between the set changes I await in transition for a small voice to whisper, "you're on in 5," "places please" or "go." That gets me ready to go on for my script to be flipped to show my worst critics, even though you planned evil against me God had planned good to come out of it. God's my script flipper, let him flip yours and see how he'll give you hope for a future that has an expected end." – A Poem by Joel Brown

There's this scripture in the Bible that says,

"Who has saved us, and called us with an holy calling, not according to our works, but according to his own purpose and grace, which was given us in Christ Jesus before the world began. But is now by the appearing of our Savior Jesus Christ, who hath abolished death, and hath brought life and immortality to light through the gospel." – 2 Timothy 1:9-10

"Just because you face death doesn't mean it stings, even when the sting has been removed as hurting with hope still hurts. However, we can always look at pain and see power as pain is a microphone, because the more it hurts; the louder it gets. So, our pain can be an opportunity that allows us to be used by God like never before." – Paraphrased quote by Levi Lusko

In fact, you can have peace of mind and live with

this expectancy that you don't have to be scared to death of death, or of dying. Thus, through Jesus Christ; you can become a new creature, immortal, and absolutely incapable of death – imagine that, a fresh start with immortality.

But let me explain this further through a devotion that I once read called, 'From faith to faith: a daily guide to victory' by Gloria and Kenneth Copeland who put it this way.

Death. It's not a popular topic – even among believer. In fact, a great many are just plain scared of it. Oh yes, they talk about having eternal life. Yet when the devil tries to threaten their earthly survival with sickness or calamity, they panic.

Why? Because they haven't learned to look at death through God's eyes. Even though their spirit has been made immortal, they haven't renewed their minds to include that truth. If they had, when the devil tried to push their panic button, they'd just laugh and say, 'You can't scare me. Devil, I've done all the dying I'm ever going to do!" That's true, you know. The Word of God says that you, as a born-again believer, are never going to see death (John 8:51).

Jesus has been your substitute. He suffered death, so you wouldn't have to. And He was raised, Hebrews 2:14-15 says, "Destroy[ing] him that had the power of death, that is, the devil, and deliver[ed] them who through fear of death wear all their lifetime subject to bondage." If you've made Jesus the Lord of your life, the only death you'll ever experience is behind you now. It occurred the instant you received Christ.

At that moment, your old self – the one whose nature was to sin and rebel against God – died. Your body didn't die, but your spirit man – the real you – died to Satan and all of his works. You became "a new Creature" (2 Corinthians 5:17), immortal and absolutely incapable of death!

When you're finished with your work on the earth, you're not going to die. You'll simply shed your earthly shell and relocate to a far more glorious place. Go to the Word and get God's perspective on death. Make a study of it. Once the reality of your immortality begins to dawn on you, the devil will never be able to threaten you with it again." Said Gloria Copeland – 'No More Dying to Do' devotional.

Read the scripture in Hebrews 2:9-18.

And if you would like to accept this invitation of salvation that only Jesus Christ can give with hope in your own horror story that you might be walking through, then I'd like to invite you to follow these steps to begin your journey to peace and eternal assurance.

STEP 1
God loves you and has a plan for you!

The Bible says, "God so loved the world that

He gave His one and only Son, [Jesus Christ], that whoever believes in Him shall not perish, but have eternal life" (John 3:16).

Jesus said, "I came that they may have life and have it abundantly" — a complete life full of purpose (John 10:10).

STEP 2

Here's the problem: man is sinful and separated from God.

We have all done, thought or said bad things, which the Bible calls "sin." The Bible says, "All have sinned and fall short of the glory of God" (Romans 3:23).

The result of sin is death, spiritual separation from God (Romans 6:23).

And, the good news?

STEP 3

God sent His Son to die for your sins!

Jesus died in our place so we could have a relationship with God and be with Him forever.

"God demonstrates His own love toward us, in that while we were yet sinners, Christ died for us" (Romans 5:8).

But it didn't end with His death on the cross. He rose again and still lives!

"Christ died for our sins... He was buried. ... He was raised on the third day, according to the Scriptures" (1 Cor. 15:3-4).

Jesus is the only way to God. Jesus said, "I am the way, and the truth, and the life; no one comes to the Father, but through Me" (John 14:6).

STEP 4

Would you like to receive God's forgiveness?

We can't earn salvation; we are saved by God's grace when we have faith in His Son, Jesus Christ.

All you have to do is believe you are a sinner that Christ died for your sins and ask His forgiveness.

Then turn from your sins—that's called repentance. Jesus Christ knows you and loves you. What matters to Him is the attitude of your heart, your honesty. We suggest praying the prayer below to accept Christ as your Savior.

PRAY NOW

"Dear God, I know I'm a sinner, and I ask for your forgiveness. I believe Jesus Christ is Your Son. I believe that He died for my sin and that you raised Him to life. I want to trust Him as my Savior and follow Him as Lord, from this day forward. Guide my life and help me to do your will. I pray this in the name of Jesus. Amen."

RESOURCE: peacewithgod.net

THE NEXT STEPS:
- Begin reading the Bible - youversion.com
- Know Jesus - a free, guided online course shows you what it means to have faith in Christ and how to communicate with Him. courses.goingfarther.net/know-jesus
- Find a church - search for a church - churches.goingfarther.net
- Life Issues - a practical direction for moving forward with difficult life situations - goingfarther.net/life-issues
- Basics of Christianity - a place to learn more about what Christians believe - goingfarther.net/basics-of-christianity
- One Minute Apologetics gives you credible answers to the curious questions you seek – oneminuteapologist.com

RECEIVING THE HOLY SPIRIT

An impartation to receive the powers of the Holy Spirit who will help you to do 'Spiritual Combat' against any battle you will face in life and show you how to live victorious of it.

One very effective strategy is speaking in tongues – an ethereal prayer language that utters mysteries unto God that no men or demon can understand.

Nevertheless, it's an act of spiritual warfare for intercession that gives someone the ability to allow the Holy Spirit to pray through you when you don't know what to pray.

Another thing that the Holy Spirit does for you is He puts your spirit in charge, for instance, Pastor Gloria Copeland once said, "as long as you live on earth, you're going to be saddled with a weakness.

What is it? The flesh and blood body you live in. It's a body that's subject to death. For example, a body that's subject to the physical world around you. Your reborn spirit doesn't want to sin. It wants to be completely obedient to God.

But the weakness of the flesh causes you to fall prey to the temptations around you. Does that mean you're doomed to life of failure till Jesus comes and that flesh body is glorified?

No! It means you need to build your spirit up, to strengthen it, until it dominates your flesh. We are told to crucify the flesh. Your spirit by the Holy Spirit applies spirit to flesh. It causes your spirit to rise up and take charge. Just like using barbells strengthens your arms, praying in other tongues strengthens your spirit.

You see, your spirit is more powerful than your flesh, and as you give it outflow, the flesh will simply have to yield to it. Most believers don't understand that. They'll be overwhelmed by some sin, and instead of conquering it by the things of God such as praying in the spirit, they'll simply keep struggling to overcome in natural ways.

So they end up failing again and again. If you're caught in that cycle, take heart! God hasn't commanded you to be more spiritual than you can be. He knows your weakness and He's given you a way to overcome it. He's given you the ability to pray in tongues – and with your understanding to wield the sword of the Spirit, which is the Word of God. And no matter how badly you're falling in everything else, you can do these things!

Be warned though, Satan will try to talk you out of it. He knows that once you learn how to bring the flesh in line, he'll have no foothold left in your life. You'll shut the door on him and he won't be able to get in."

With the Holy Spirit in you-you can overpower any darkness that surrounds you; His power is superpower.

To learn more about the Holy Spirit who is a divine friend and so much more, please read Romans 8 and go to - thebibleproject.com/explore/holy-spirit

With that said, I want to extend the invitation to receive the Holy Spirit.

Other than that in pertaining to the Holy Spirit, a Pastor by the name of Andrew Wommack has said that "As His child, your loving heavenly Father wants to give you the supernatural power you need to live this new life."

"For every one that asketh receiveth; and he that seeketh findeth; and to him that knocketh it shall be opened...how much more shall your heavenly Father give the Holy Spirit to them that ask him?" (Luke 11:10-13).

"All you have to do is ask, believe, and receive" (ref. Wommack)!

"Pray: 'Father, I recognize my need for Your power to live this new life. Please fill me with Your Holy Spirit. By faith, I receive it right now! Thank you for baptizing me! Holy Spirit, You are welcome in my life'" (ref. Wommack)!

Congratulations – now you're filled with God's supernatural power! Some syllables from a language you don't recognize will rise up from your heart to your mouth (1 Corinthians 14:14).

"As you speak them out loud by faith, you're releasing God's power from within and building yourself up in the spirit (1 Corinthians 14:4). You can do this whenever and wherever you like" (ref. Wommack)!

"It doesn't really matter whether you felt anything or not when you prayed to receive the Lord and His Spirit. If you believed in your heart that you received, the God's Word promises you did. 'Therefore I say unto you, what things soever ye desire, when ye pray, believe that ye receive them, and ye shall have them' (Mark

11:24). God always honors His Word – believe it" (ref. Wommack)!

Now please go to - peacewithgod.net - and send them messages, letting them know that you've prayed to receive Jesus as your Savior. So they can rejoice with you and help you understand more fully what has taken place in your life, as I believe they'll send you a free gift that will help you understand and grow in your new relationship with the Lord. Welcome to your new life!

ABOUT THE AUTHOR

Paper writes when I think. This pen bleeds words out in ink. Take it in, breath it out. Creating characters, like dropping a Deus ex machina, giving them a voice to speak. Now, what am I? A Story.

The Art of giving is to be in service as a Writer, through my craft I have the ability to inspire change in people; its a tool to change people's out-look and to give them something to better themselves with as I also get to Connect with People, Walk in their Shoe, and Flip-the-Script to change the scene for a day in hope that it might change the outcome that might be bad to turn it around for the good with a personalized sci-fi short-story.

To get the person's mind off the matter and in a created atmosphere of faith that would allow them to believe in something more; to provide good public relations. There is something about Joel that can't be put on paper, the bottom line he has, what it takes to make a difference in the world.

Joel Brown is an extremely passionate and creative activist who loves being a voice for

unidentified missing kids as an invisible
dancer with OCD/ADHD, and fanfic flash-
fiction protest artist for missing kids.

Joel is looking to find a hurt to heal and a need
to fill in adoption and missing kids' advocacy as
a CRIME-FIGHTER-WRITER, with the eventual
opportunity of progressive growth toward a career
interest in the field of Arts & Communications
and Intelligence Analyst. Joel Brown lives
in Tulsa, Oklahoma with his mother.

After withdrawing from a private University
due to financial difficulties with just two credits
away from being able to graduate with a Bachelor
of Science degree in Drama, Television and Film
Performance; he dived into working and living
doing what he loved most - writing and registered
to become a Christian ordained minister.

He has designed and created the Akterpuz third-
arm StomoArt that is hand crafted. Which is an
artsy-craftsy, severed Martian arm for holding
movie refreshments and an actor's script that
is a mobile, handy, adjustable, convenient,
multipurpose device that offers a third-arm
that extends a extra hand to movie-lovers.

He has studied Computer Information System:
Digital Video, Photography, Practical Ministry
Film Analysis, Positive Psychology, certified in
Cinema a Therapy, curated a collection of movies
on DVD, traveled to Beverly Hills, California in

order to record a demo in a collaboration with a top notch underground Hip-hop artist and producer—all while studying and experiencing more than 23 years' worth of knowledge on music, dance, filmmaking and acting.

However, it wasn't until after he went through a major life trauma that narrowed down his Jack-of-all-trades pursuit into a master-of-one calling, where it was led to a story that had filmed in film school but shelved for 18-years and stayed up at all hours of the night crafting it into a book, Brown wrote Picasso's Little Secret: The Devil's Paintbrush, a series of novels whose first installment is Painting Shadows. The elaborate story continues with the much-anticipated Part Two: Painting Shadow Town, and even an expected Part Three, Four and Five.

Despite that Brown strives to leave a legacy that will be known as a 'MAN-ON-FIRE FOR WRITING AND MOVIES WHO'S AFTER GOD'S OWN HEART' who God had another word for him: REDEEMED and a FATHER'S HEART, when the world labeled him repulsively that set apart before all as a display of God's gracious merciful power.

Thus, regardless of how insurmountable the situations he faces may look, he kept on doing what he loved, and they didn't take away his passion but made his fight stronger as an artist. Your word-serving pen-pushing imagineer writer, Joel Brown AKA: Joel Flickstein.